DISCOVER

The Cotswolds

CONTENTS

MYRIAD

Around Cheltenham and Gloucester

The western edge of the Cotswolds is dominated by a large escarpment – the Cotswold edge – and by the mighty river Severn and its tributaries which flow down from the surrounding hills. The river has carved out deep and wide valleys and it is on these that the prosperous towns of Cheltenham and Gloucester are situated. The Severn estuary gives access to the sea and for centuries Gloucester was a major port for the west of England. There are dramatic views all along the edge of the escarpment – such as those at Crickley Hill, shown below.

Cheltenham During the Regency period, Cheltenham Spa rivalled Bath in its splendour as the rich and fashionable came to take the waters. Much of the layout of today's town dates from this period. Cheltenham retains many of its fine Regency features such as spacious squares, crescents, terraces, promenades and beautifully laid out formal gardens. These are to be found on either side of the striking tree-lined Promenade. The source of Cheltenham's wealth can be seen in its neo-classical Pittville Pump Room complete with an elegant circular bandstand. As well as horse-racing Cheltenham hosts several major festivals each year, including those devoted to music, science and literature.

▼ **Cleeve Common** Cleeve Hill and Cleeve Common form a broad expanse of gently sloping open countryside just to the north-east of Cheltenham. West Down is located on Cleeve Common – at 1082ft (330m), it is the Cotswolds' highest point. Magnificent views over the Severn Vale and the Malvern Hills are easily accessible from the scarp slope that rises out of Cheltenham. The area is popular with walkers and riders and there is plenty of wildlife to observe in addition to the more traditional Cotswold cattle and sheep. The common was an important grazing area during the Middle Ages and an earthwork known as the Ring provides evidence of Roman live-stock husbandry.

▲▶ **Sudeley Castle** Sudeley Castle has had a chequered history. There was a castle on the site in Norman times but this was rebuilt in 1442 by Ralph Boteler. In the Tudor period the castle became the home of Katherine Parr, the last wife of Henry VIII, and in the Civil War it was Prince Rupert's head-quarters. Sudeley then fell into disrepair until it was acquired by the Dent family in 1837. Extensive restorations were carried out under Lady Emma Dent. Katherine Parr had married Thomas Seymour after the death of Henry VIII but she later died in childbirth. A portrait of Katherine and a love letter written by her to Thomas Seymour are preserved at the castle and her marble tomb in the chapel was designed by Sir Gilbert Scott.

▶▼ **Winchcombe** Sheltered on three sides by pleasantly wooded hills, the unspoilt town of Winchcombe is tucked away into the Cotswold edge. It was one of the seats of the Saxon kings of Mercia and was later a county town until it was absorbed by Gloucestershire. In the Middle Ages its abbey was a place of pilgrimage for followers of the martyred St Kenelm. The abbey has now completely disappeared. Most of the buildings that distinguish the town today are largely the legacy of the Cotswold wool trade. The town also benefited from its proximity to Sudeley Castle when the castle was the seat of great magnates and a host for royal visits.

▶ **Cooper's Hill** Every spring bank holiday Monday, Cooper's Hill, which juts into the Severn Vale, is the scene of a cheese-rolling race in which competitors pursue seven-pound local cheeses (strengthened with discs of wood) down a one-in-two slope.

▼ **Leckhampton** At the end of the 18th century local landowner Brandon Trye developed quarries in Leckhampton, now a suburb of Cheltenham, and built a horse-drawn railway to transport the stone. One particularly hard pillar of rock left untouched by the quarrymen is known as the Devil's Chimney.

▲▶ Gloucester Built mainly on the eastern bank of the river Severn and dating back to Roman times, Gloucester is sheltered by the Cotswolds to the east, by the Forest of Dean to the west and protected by the Malvern Hills to the north-west. Gloucester's cathedral has its origins in an abbey founded in 681 and is the burial place of King Edward II, who was murdered at nearby Berkeley Castle. In the Middle Ages it was a centre for pilgrimage. Gloucester's long and prosperous history as a trading centre, inland port and spa can be glimpsed in the many fine buildings and churches that adorn the city.

▲▶ **Gloucester Docks** The docks were opened in 1827 and gave direct access by seagoing ships to Gloucester via the Severn estuary and a ship canal. At the docks goods could be transferred to canal barges for transportation throughout the Midlands. The docks and warehouses were further expanded in 1848 to cope with increased corn imports following the repeal of the Corn Laws. By the 1980s most commercial traffic had died away and the docks now provide spacious accommodation and ample leisure facilities. The survival of the old warehouses makes the main basin a popular location for filming period drama; fans of *The Onedin Line* will recognise Biddle's warehouse where many episodes of the seafaring drama were filmed.

▲ Withington The manor of Withington was formerly held by the bishops of Worcester and several of its buildings date back to the 15th century. The Mill Inn has the river Coln running through its gardens, although the water wheel has now disappeared. At the centre of the village is a well-preserved church with many Norman features including a solid tower and splendid south doorway. A large Roman villa once stood in the area and a mosaic pavement from it is now in the British Museum.

▼ Hawling Situated in the high sheep country Hawling provides walkers with many pleasant routes that offer extensive views over the surrounding area. One popular walk follows a bridleway from the village to Deadmanbury Gate on the western edge of Guiting woods. The village is small and quiet with a handsome Elizabethan manor house next to its church. The church was largely rebuilt in 1764 and has a Georgian pulpit and an interesting set of 17th century brass plaques.

Naunton The village of Naunton lies in the upper Windrush valley and has been a centre for sheep-rearing since the area became monastic land in the Middle Ages. This long history of animal husbandry means that this part of the Windrush valley is home to flowers such as cowslips, yellow rattle and orchids found only on unimproved limestone pasture. Naunton's other industry was the production of stone roofing slates; at one time 30,000 a week were dug from thin stone seams in nearby mines. The church has an imposing Perpendicular tower complete with pinnacles and gargoyles.

Inside there is a carved 15th century stone pulpit and a font from about the same period. Naunton's dovecote (right) erected in 1660 incorporates four gables round a central turret. It has 1,176 nest holes for doves kept for winter food.

Hazleton Located in the heart of the Cotswolds, between Cirencester and Stow-on-the-Wold, Hazleton's high position gives excellent views over the surrounding countryside. Its relative isolation means that the village has changed little in recent years but the Salt Way, a medieval path used by mules to carry salt down from the mines in Cheshire to Lechlade, once passed through the village. Hazleton prospered during the later medieval period as

a result of the wool trade. The parish church is a Norman foundation but its tower and windows belong to the later Perpendicular period. The south doorway and chancel arch are Norman and there is a very solid 13th century baptismal font. As in ancient times there is a great deal of foot and horse traffic around the village and excellent bridleways to Salperton in the north, Notgrove to the north-east and Turkdean to the east.

Guiting Power Lying near the confluence of the river Windrush and one of its tributaries, the name Guiting Power is derived from a mixture of the Old English word *gyte*, which means an outpouring of water, and the name of the Le Poer family, the village's 13th century owners. The majority of houses in Guiting Power are clustered around a sloping village green with the war memorial at its centre.

Around Cirencester

The open limestone countryside of the Cotswolds made the area attractive to Iron Age farmers as it was relatively easy to plough. In the Middle Ages improved horse plough technology made lowland areas more accessible and the Cotswolds became one of the country's prime sheep-rearing centres. English wool was a highly valued commodity and Cotswold towns and villages grew rich on its trade. Crops ripen slowly on this upland farming land – as a well-known Gloucestershire proverb says, it's "as slow in coming as Cotswold barley".

Cirencester This was an important city during the Roman era and stood at the junction of three major roads: the Fosse Way, the Ermin Way and Akeman Street. Today the only visible remains of the Roman city are part of the old town wall and a large turf-covered amphitheatre. The town's prosperity in the Middle Ages was aided by the presence of a large abbey and it eventually grew to pre-eminence in the wool trade. At the centre of Cirencester is its marketplace which even in the 21st century retains a great deal of the atmosphere of a prosperous Cotswold wool town. Rising above the marketplace is the 162ft (49m) high Perpendicular tower of its parish church – the largest in Gloucestershire.

Cirencester Park
Occupying 3000 acres, Cirencester Park, now famous as a polo ground, was laid out geometrically according to Baroque ideas about landscaping. The park was begun by the first Earl Bathurst in 1714-18 and is still part of the Bathurst estate. The earl introduced the hexagon, a Doric column surmounted with a statue of Queen Anne and the Gothic folly of Alfred's Hall.

▲▼ The Ampneys This small group of villages lie, as their name suggests, on the Ampney Brook. Each has its own church and each village was a thriving community during the Middle Ages. The original parish of Ampney St Mary has disappeared making its church seem isolated. The present Ampney St Mary was formerly known as the hamlet of Ashbrook. The church of St Mary is a small Norman structure that still preserves many fascinating original features such as a carved lintel and medieval wall paintings. The church of the Holy Rood (*rood* being an Anglo-Saxon word for cross) gives Ampney Crucis its name and there is a rare 15th century cross in its grounds. This was hidden from 17th century Puritans by being walled up inside the building. The third village in the group is Ampney St Peter. Its church is mostly Saxon in design with some Victorian additions and there is a carved pre-Christian fertility symbol in the grounds. The largest house in the area is Ampney Park which was originally constructed for the Pleydell family in 1561; its extremely well-preserved Jacobean ceiling is particularly noteworthy.

Chedworth Eleven miles south-east of Cheltenham, Chedworth combines the ancient and modern. Opposite the ancient Seven Tuns Inn a spring emerges from a wall whilst elsewhere in the village there is a sculpture of the Virgin and Child carved by Helen Rock in 1911. The church retains some Norman features but it has been sensitively added to over the centuries. Not far from the village is Chedworth Roman villa. Discovered in 1864 and dating from AD120-400, the beautifully preserved remains include mosaic pavements (one depicting the four seasons), bath suites and a hypocaust. There is a small museum near the site.

Bibury dates back to Saxon times but the bulk of the village owes its existence to the 17th century wool trade. Arlington Row (left) is an ancient terrace of weavers' cottages. Rack Isle, in front of the cottages and now a nature reserve, was originally used for drying wool. Alongside the traditional wool bale tombs in Bibury churchyard can be found Bisley Piece. This was established in the 14th century when the people of Bisley angered a pope. Forbidden to bury their dead in Bisley, they had to travel 15 miles to use this tiny graveyard instead.

Northleach This was one of the most important Cotswold wool towns in the Middle Ages and its heyday as a medieval trading centre can still be glimpsed in its market square and many half-timbered buildings. The most obvious legacy of Northleach's pre-eminence in the wool trade is its church. This was largely rebuilt in the Perpendicular style in the 15th century and is a magnificent example of the style and period. The pinnacled south porch is said to be without equal in England and the tower combines both elegance and strength. The generous windows in the clerestory provide ample light for such features as a 15th century goblet-shaped pulpit and a new ceiling designed by Sir Basil Spence. The church also has an extensive collection of brasses which commemorate the wool merchants whose wealth made the rebuilding and remodelling of the church possible.

▲ **North Cerney** A single street with views across the Churn valley is the extent of this idyllic village. The church with its saddleback tower was largely rebuilt in the 1470s following a fire but it retains some Norman features. The interior is said to be one of the best furnished in England and has a finely carved stone pulpit. The churchyard contains a well-restored 14th century cross and some unusual 16th century graffiti on the exterior wall; one carving seems to be of a mythical beast, with a lion's head and tail but the body of a man, known as a manticore. The primary school was founded in 1844 and there is also a Methodist chapel dating from 1891. The large lime tree on the village green marks the site of Methodist camp meetings in the 19th and early 20th centuries.

◀ **The Duntisbournes** The four villages that bear the name Duntisbourne are strung out in a line along the Dun Brook. They are: Duntisbourne Abbots, Duntisbourne Leer, Duntisbourne Rouse and Middle Duntisbourne. Only Duntisbourne Abbots and Duntisbourne Rouse have churches. Today, Duntisbourne Leer is little more than a couple of farmhouses by a ford. The more interesting of the churches is the tiny church of Saint Michael in Duntisbourne Rouse. It has a Saxon nave and, because of the sloping ground, a small crypt chapel beneath the Norman chancel – which is unusual in such a small church.

North Cotswolds

Regarded by many as the true heart of the region, the northern Cotswolds contain classic locations such as Stow-on-the-Wold, Moreton-in-Marsh, Chipping Campden and Broadway. Wool production made these towns prosperous and it was this trade which paid for the great houses, the massive Perpendicular churches and even the labourers' cottages that you can see today. At Snowshill (below), just above the town of Broadway, sheep still graze as they have done for centuries.

▲ **Stow-on-the-Wold** This pretty market centre has the dubious distinction of being the highest town, at 800ft (244m), in the Cotswolds. A popular rhyme begins, "Stow-on-the-Wold, where the wind blows cold". Despite its position, Stow-on-the-Wold has been a thriving market town since at least 1107 when it received its first royal charter. There were two annual fairs by the 15th century and Daniel Defoe reported the sale of 20,000 sheep in a day there in the 18th century. In later years Stow-on-the-Wold became famous for its horse fairs, but nowadays the only horses at the two charter fairs, one held in May and one in October, are likely to be on the merry-go-rounds.

▲ **Lower Slaughter** At one end of Lower Slaughter is a large millpond which feeds a working water wheel. The 19th century mill – the Old Mill – with its distinctive tall redbrick chimney is open to the public and houses a museum. The village hall was built in 1887 and provides a late Victorian attempt at a traditional Cotswold style. Also dating from the 19th century is St Mary's church which was rebuilt in 1867. It has an imposing spire and some 13th century arches from the original church between the nave and south aisle.

▼ **Moreton-in-Marsh** Situated on the watershed between the Thames and the Severn, the town straddles the Fosse Way and its position accounts for its prosperity. During the 17th and 18th centuries it was on the main coaching route between London, Oxford, Worcester and Hereford. When coaching declined the town quickly moved on to railways; the Stratford-Moreton tramway opened in 1826 and was one of the earliest in the country. A mainline service arrived in 1843 and the line between London, Oxford and Worcester was opened in 1853. As a centre for travellers Moreton-in-Marsh is well provided with inns one of which, the 16th century White Hart (Royal) Hotel, was used by Charles I during the Civil War. The Curfew Tower on the corner of Oxford Street still has its original 1633 curfew bell. Chastleton House, three miles south-east of the town, is a fine Jacobean manor house which still contains much of its original furniture; it is now run by the National Trust. Two miles from Moreton-in-Marsh is the Four Shires Stone, a Cotswold stone pillar that marked the coming together of the four counties of Gloucestershire, Worcestershire, Oxfordshire and Warwickshire. Unfortunately county boundary changes have left the stone out of date.

◀ **Hidcote** The tiny hamlet of Hidcote Bartrim is famous for the National Trust owned gardens of Hidcote Manor. The 17th century Hidcote Manor was acquired in 1907 by the family of Major Lawrence Johnston. At that time its gardens consisted of little more than a few fields but once Johnston became interested they quickly grew in both size and scope so that by the 1920s Johnston employed 12 full-time gardeners. Rather than laying out a single garden Johnston laid out a series of them separated by walls and trees.

▼ **Blockley** Thanks to the power of Blockley Brook the village was one of the first in England to produce its own electricity. In previous centuries the brook provided the energy for corn mills, silk throwers and even wood saws. Six mills once operated in the village although only one is still open; the beautiful Mill Dene garden has been created around another one. Parts of the church date from the Norman period but the tower was only added in 1725 by local quarry owner Thomas Woodward. Inside the church is a series of handsome monuments to local landowners.

▲◀ **Chipping Campden** The word "chipping" relates to an Old English word meaning market and it was as a wool and cattle market that the town first grew up. Grevel House was built for William Grevel in about 1380 and features striking Perpendicular-style two storey windows. The market hall (left) was built in 1627. The row of almshouses just below St James' church dates from 1612. Next to the church are the lodges and gateway to Campden House. These are some of the only remains of the original buildings as the rest were burned down during the Civil War. St James' church is a significant local landmark. It is built in the Perpendicular style and its interior houses some interesting marble monuments.

▲ **Broadway** With its handsome main street, Broadway is regarded by many as the finest large village in the Cotswolds; it was once an important staging post on the London to Worcester route. A new turnpike road was opened in 1736 and at one time seven coaches passed through the village each day. Many of the fine buildings along the main street began their lives as inns to serve the passing trade. With the coming of the railways the coach trade died away but Broadway had its own station and it quickly became a stopping off point for exploration of the Cotswolds. It was a favourite of William Morris and other members of the Arts & Crafts movement.

◀ **Laverton** A hamlet located beneath the Cotswold edge, Laverton contains several substantial and well-built farmhouses that date back to the 16th century and make good use of local stone. Laverton is close to the Cotswold Way and the many fine views in the area make it popular with walkers. Broadway to the north and Stanton to the south are within easy reach.

▶ **Stanton** Most of the houses in Stanton date from the 17th century. The village was extensively restored by the architect Sir Philip Stott after he purchased large tracts of it just before the First World War. He modernised many features but set up covenants to prevent the worst excesses of the 20th century from taking hold. His work means that Stanton often provides a backdrop for period film and television dramas. Parts of the church date back to the 12th century and it features both a 14th century and a Jacobean pulpit. It has an elegant spire and some of its windows are from the 15th century. Stanton is claimed by many to be one of the oldest villages in the Cotswolds.

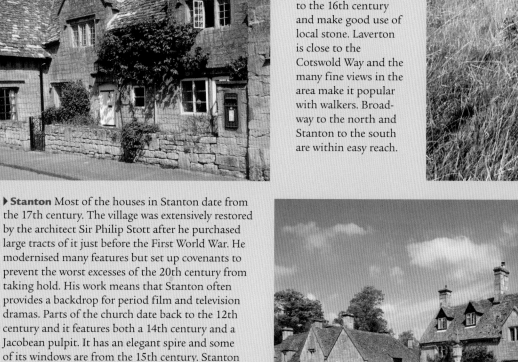

▲ Stanway The village of Stanway is dominated by the gatehouse to Stanway House. The house was built during the 1580s on the site of an earlier manor house. The grounds contain a restored water garden featuring the highest fountain in England, a tithe barn dating from 1370 and a log-fired brewing house. Opposite the driveway to Stanway House is a thatched cricket pavilion mounted on saddle stones. This unusual building was a gift to the village by the author of *Peter Pan*, J M Barrie.

▼ Snowshill This pretty villlage was owned by Winchcombe Abbey from 821 until the Dissolution of the Monasteries when it was given to King Henry VIII's wife Katherine Parr. In 1919 the almost derelict manor house was restored by Charles Paget Wade, as a place to present his collection of 22,000 examples of craftsmanship. Amassed between 1900 and 1951 the collection includes automatons, butter stamps, bicycles, children's toys, clocks, cowbells, locks and 26 suits of Samurai armour.

▲ Saintbury Ranged along the side of Saintbury Hill, the Norman church in Saintbury still preserves some fragments of a former Saxon building. The village itself features a fine cross which stands at the crossroads to the north of the village. The lower part dates from the 15th century whilst the Maltese cross and sundial were added in 1848.

South Cotswolds

The Cotswold escarpment stretches south-west as far as Bath where the beautiful cream-coloured limestone of the buildings has helped to add classical dignity and splendour to the fine Georgian architecture of the city. South Cotswold villages such as Marshfield and Castle Combe have a different ambience to those in the North Cotswolds but their buildings are created from the same materials and the lanes and surrounding countryside are full of Cotswolds' charm.

◆ **Bath** is a city that has had two major heydays. The first was during the Roman occupation when the town of *Aquae Sulis* grew up around the natural hot springs in the area; the second was during the Regency and Georgian periods when the craze for taking the waters made Bath the centre of fashion and one of the largest cities in England. The Roman temple and baths, the abbey and the city's famous crescents are all built from locally quarried limestone. The 18th century spa town was largely built in the Classical style with long stretches of identical façades to give impressions of palatial scale and classical decorum.

▼ **Castle Combe** The village is centred on a market cross that reflects its growth through wool trading. Other marks of this once-great industry include several fine timber-framed buildings clustered around the cross and the substantial Perpendicular tower that was added to the church in 1434. The village is situated on the By Brook with a charming bridge that spans the stream.

▼ Tetbury Dominating Tetbury is its 17th century Market House. This imposing building is supported on three rows of pillars and has a stone roof; it used to be even higher but it was reduced by one storey in 1817. Above the roof is a fine cupola on which there is a weather vane decorated with gilded dolphins. The dolphins also appear on the town's coat of arms. Near to the Market House are the Chipping Steps, where a livestock market was formerly held amongst an imposing collection of 18th and 19th century buildings. Also in this area is Gumstool Hill where the annual Woolsack Races take place every spring bank holiday Monday. This gruelling event involves contestants running down Gumstool Hill (one-in-four) and up again carrying a 60lb (27kg) woolsack. Teams of young men and women – the women's sacks are only 35lb (16kg) – take part in the race whilst townspeople dress up in medieval costumes. In 1633 the town was sold to four local residents who became known as the Feoffees. Along with 13 town wardens the Feoffees virtually ran Tetbury; today they confine themselves to charitable activities. St Mary's church is an imposing building rebuilt in the Gothic style in the late 18th century. Tetbury's original courthouse now houses a Police Museum.

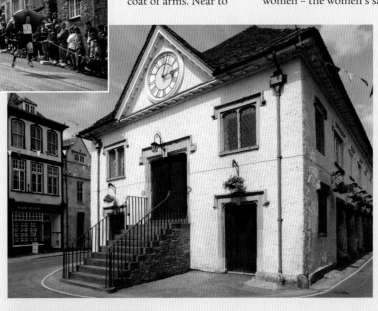

◄▼ Hawkesbury The village of Hawkesbury, which nestles in a wooded coombe below the Cotswold escarpment, is dominated by its church which dates back to the 12th century and is on the site of an earlier Saxon church. It is mainly in the Perpendicular style. The Old Vicarage to the east of the church is an unusual L-shape and dates from the late 15th century. It features a two storey gabled porch and a late 18th century garden building with Gothic arched windows. Outside the village on the Cotswold edge is the Somerset Monument, erected in 1846 to commemorate General Lord Edward Somerset who served with distinction at Waterloo and died in 1842. Somerset was the nephew of the sixth Duke of Beaufort whose family home is at nearby Badminton. The slightly tapering square tower (left) is approximately 100ft (30m) high and is a well-known local landmark. The 102 mile (164km) long-distance footpath, the Cotswold Way, passes near the village.

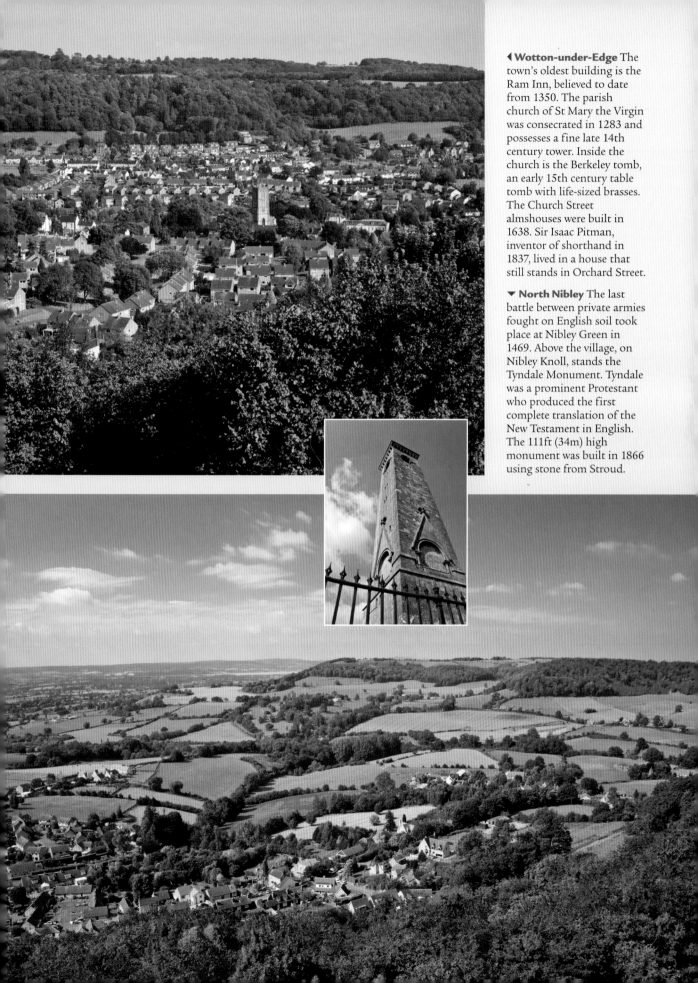

◀ **Wotton-under-Edge** The town's oldest building is the Ram Inn, believed to date from 1350. The parish church of St Mary the Virgin was consecrated in 1283 and possesses a fine late 14th century tower. Inside the church is the Berkeley tomb, an early 15th century table tomb with life-sized brasses. The Church Street almshouses were built in 1638. Sir Isaac Pitman, inventor of shorthand in 1837, lived in a house that still stands in Orchard Street.

▼ **North Nibley** The last battle between private armies fought on English soil took place at Nibley Green in 1469. Above the village, on Nibley Knoll, stands the Tyndale Monument. Tyndale was a prominent Protestant who produced the first complete translation of the New Testament in English. The 111ft (34m) high monument was built in 1866 using stone from Stroud.

East Cotswolds

The undulating countryside of the east Cotswolds contains many gems: the fine market town of Burford and the watery delights of towns such as Bourton-on-the-Water on the river Windrush, the village of Sherborne, close to the Sherborne Brook (below) and Eastleach on the river Leach. This area may not have the high escarpments and dramatic views of the Cotswold edge but its pretty villages and riverside walks make it a firm favourite with visitors.

Burford The eastern gateway to the Cotswolds, Burford built its reputation on wool, quarrying and coaching. Stone from quarries near the town was used in the construction of some of Britain's finest buildings, from Blenheim Palace to St Paul's cathedral. Burford's heyday as a coaching town came in the 18th century when it was an important stop on routes into Oxford and London; "Burford Bait", the huge meals served by the inns, were legendary. The town's steep High Street with its many inns is one of the most attractive thoroughfares in the Cotswolds.

▼ **Windrush** Named after the river on which it stands, this is a former quarrying village with many fine houses built from local stone. St Peter's church is of Norman origin and has been Windrush's parish church since 1586. The south doorway is elaborately carved with menacing looking beaked heads which are mixed with the heads of other fantastical beasts. In the churchyard there is a finely decorated wool bale tomb, which represents the source of the deceased's wealth in the form of corded bales of wool.

▲ **Bledington** In the valley of the Evenlode, Bledington is built around a wide village green. The church is located to the south of the green with a charming row of cottages overlooking the churchyard. Refurbished in the 15th century out of profits from the wool trade, its interior features several 15th century Perpendicular windows containing stained glass believed to be the work of John Pruddle, the master craftsman who produced the windows of Beauchamp chapel in Warwick.

▲▶ Bourton-on-the-Water Five ornamental bridges span the river Windrush in Bourton-on-the-Water giving it a unique appeal and the nickname of the "Venice of the Cotswolds". Moving downstream, the five bridges are: Bourton Bridge built in 1806 and widened in 1959; Mill Bridge (also known as Broad Bridge) built in 1654 on the site of a former ford; High Bridge, a footbridge built in 1756; New Bridge (or Moore Bridge) built in 1911 to traverse another ford; and Coronation Bridge, built in 1953 to replace an 18th century wooden bridge. During the summer, a game of football is attempted between two of the bridges. The goalposts are set in the river and teams play using a standard football. The aim of the game is to score as many goals as possible but the general effect is to get everyone else as wet as possible. Bourton-on-the-Water is served by the parish church of St Lawrence. The only visible part of the old church is the chancel, built in 1328 by Walter de Burhton. Other attractions in the village include the Dragonfly Maze, Birdland, the Cotswolds Motor Museum and the Model Village, a ninth scale replica of Bourton-on-the Water.

▲ Eastleach Martin and Eastleach Turville

The two villages at Eastleach, Turville and Martin, face each other across the river Leach. Each village belonged to a different manor and each has its own manor house and church. The villages are connected by two bridges. One is a road bridge but the other, known as Keble's Bridge, is an unusual structure of large flat stones. It commemorates the Keble family who were lords of the manor of Eastleach Turville in the 16th century. Eastleach's two churches stand about two hundred yards apart. Eastleach Martin has the larger of the churches and its 14th century north transept is graced with three Decorated-style windows.

▶**Fairford** Sited on the river Coln, Fairford has been a market town since 1135 when Henry I granted permission for a twice-weekly market. The jewel in Fairford's crown is the magnificent church of St Mary, built from the profits of the wool trade.

Around Stroud

The intimate countryside around Stroud was made famous by the writer Laurie Lee whose novel *Cider with Rosie* describes growing up in a Cotswold village in the early years of the twentieth century. The area has a strong industrial heritage with many mills which were powered by the fast-flowing streams running off the Cotswold escarpment. Today the bustling town of Stroud is a great centre for visitors and boasts galleries, museums, bookshops and markets. Cam Long Down (below) photographed at sunset on a crisp winter's evening exemplifies the beauty of the region.

Stroud Five valleys meet at Stroud making it a natural centre for trade and transport. In the Middle Ages the town quickly established itself as a centre of the cloth industry and at the height of its prosperity there were 150 cloth mills in and around the town. Stroud was particularly famous for manufacturing the cloth used in military uniforms. The town centre has attractive narrow streets, a Tudor town hall and the area known as the Shambles where butchers were based.

Minchinhampton This attractive village, centred on its High Street and old Market Square, was once one of the most important cloth towns in the Cotswolds. It was not easily accessible by road and this has meant that it retained more of its old-fashioned charm than many similar Cotswold towns. The square is dominated by the 17th century Market House which is supported on stone pillars.

Woodchester Two miles south of Stroud, Woodchester lies in the valley of the Nailsworth stream. To the south-west is Woodchester Park which contains the ruins of a large 19th century mansion owned by William Leigh, a wealthy merchant, who bought the park in 1846. Construction began in 1858 and continued until 1870; work stopped when William Leigh died in 1873.

Slad This small village stretches out along the side of a valley north-east of Stroud. It was the childhood home of the author Laurie Lee. Life in the village in the 1920s is brilliantly evoked in Laurie Lee's autobiography *Cider With Rosie*. Slad remains remarkably unspoiled and it is still possible to gain a sense of the quiet pre-motor car village described by Laurie Lee in the 1920s. Lee's "local", The Woolpack inn, mentioned in the book, is still trading. Laurie Lee is buried in the graveyard of Holy Trinity church in the village.

▲ **Miserden** Six miles north-east of Stroud, this ancient parish has buildings from many periods including a ruined castle and dower house. Close to the village lie the earthworks of a motte and bailey castle which was erected shortly after the Norman Conquest. The two-storey dower house dates from the 18th century and had an east wing added in the 1860s by Sir John Rolt; Sir John also rebuilt other parts of the village. The church has late Saxon origins although it was extensively restored in the 1880s. The war memorial was designed by Sir Edwin Lutyens who also carried out work at Misarden Park, a large Elizabethan mansion with exquisite gardens just to the east of the village. A comparatively recent feature is a small octagonal shelter built around a large sycamore tree.